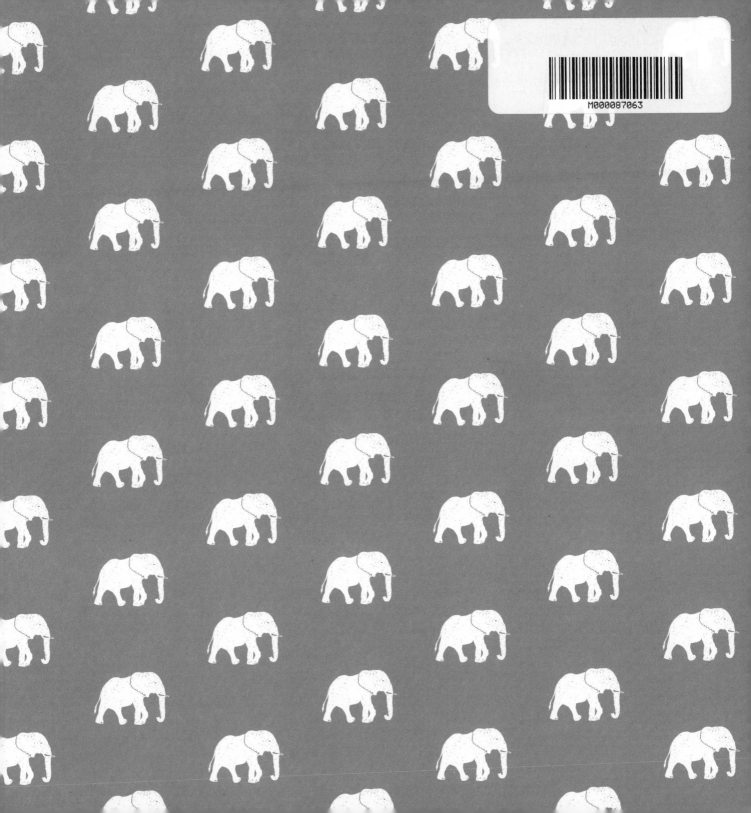

A BOY and His ELEPHANT

ETHAN L.
WATSON

Illustrations by
JESSICA K.
TALBOT

Dedicated to Nicole,
the love of my life.

Special thanks to Paul
Parkinson.

Published by Weave Media

Hardcover ISBN: 978-1-64688-000-3

Cover and book design by David Miles

First Edition

Printed in the United States

A note from the author:

When I was younger, I experienced times of frustration and discouragement because everyone around me seemed to already have intimate relationships with God, while I was still searching for my connection to Him. I eventually was able to build my knowledge of Him and form my own connection to our Father in Heaven. I learned that everyone has a unique relationship to God, and we all come to know Him through our own special way. I encourage all to seek Him, and you will find Him on your own time and in your own special way.

Best,

Ethan Watson

How are you?

Sad.

Sadness is like a thunderstorm. It comes on strong, the thunder like big feelings, the lightning like sharp pain, and the rain like the tears that follow.

I don't like rain.

I like it when I'm thirsty.

That's not helpful, El.

I'm thirsty.

When someone says they are sad, you're supposed to ask why, El.

Oh.

Why are you sad?

I don't
know God.

Who does?

My mom, my dad, my grandpa, my aunt, my teacher, the librarian, the garbage man, and that one girl from school.

Oh. How do
they know Him?

They say they hear
Him. And feel Him.

Well, that's perfect.

El, how is
that perfect?

I can't see all that well, but I have huge ears to hear, and I have a huge trunk to feel. I can help you find God.

Thanks, El.
I love you.

Jump on.
Let's go find Him.

This flower is
so beautiful.

I know.

This meadow is
so peaceful.

I know.

This wind is so powerful.

I know.

The sun is
so warm.

I know.

This river is so cold.

It is thirst
quenching.

You are a kind friend, El.

I know.

When will we find Him?

You must be patient.

I have.

You have.

Are we going
home now?

Yes.

It's too bad we didn't find Him. I would sure have liked to know Him.

But you have
met Him, and
now you know
Him.

I think you're
remembering wrong, El.

I don't think that is
possible. They say I
have the best memory.

God made the
beauty you
saw today.

God brings us
peace, just like
you felt in the
meadow.

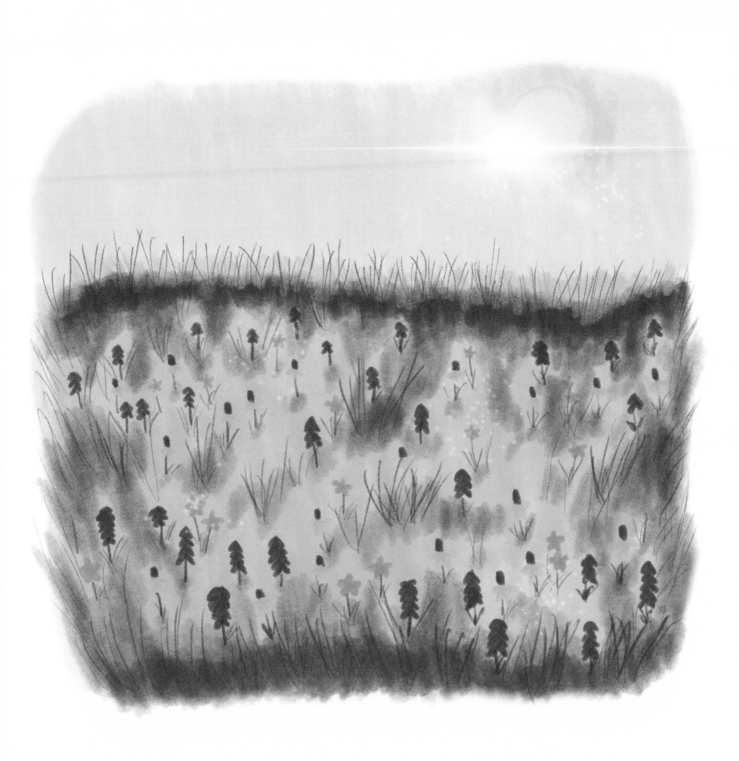

God is powerful,
just like the
strong winds of
the mountain.

God brings us
warmth in our
hearts, just like
the sun warms
our skin.

God is life
giving, just
like the river.

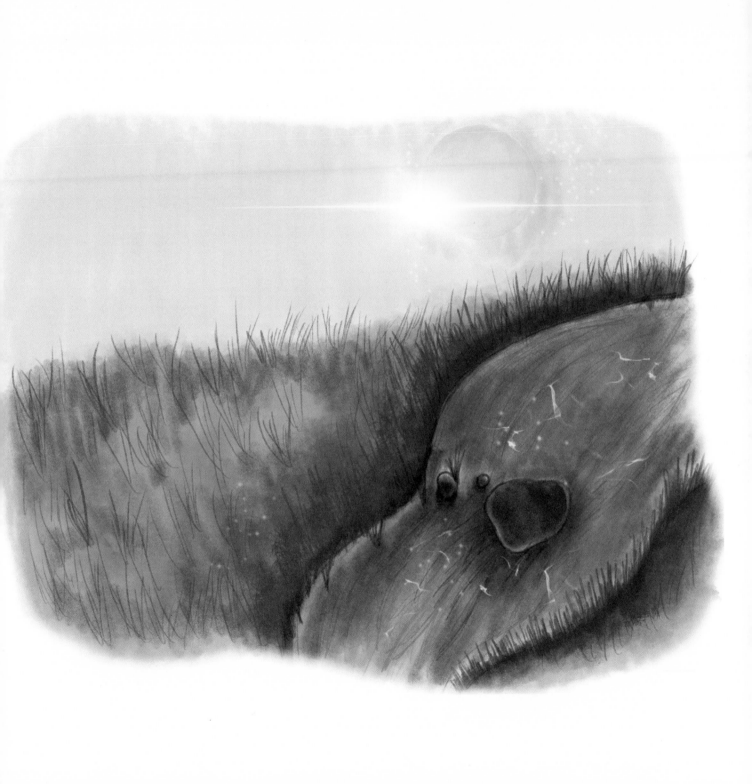

God is kind and
patient, and above
all else, He is love.

He is love. Just like you
love me, and I love you.

Wow.

I know.

I think I love God.

He loves you.

How are you now?

Happy.

My favorite part of the thunderstorm . . .

is the rainbow that follows.